A JARROLD GUIDE TO THE GEORGIAN CITY OF

BATH

Contents

Maps

Information panels

OPPOSITE **The Great
Bath and Bath Abbey**

Y0-BVN-551

BATH

For almost two thousand years Bath
has been a resort, blessed by hot springs
and the beauty of the local stone.
Today the legacy of its long
popularity is visible all around.
This World Heritage City with its
remarkable Roman baths is a gem of
Georgian elegance, with incomparable
squares and crescents climbing the
steep slopes around the city centre.

Few now travel to Bath for the curative waters, but the true enjoyment of a visit has changed little over the years. Bath has always been fun – over the centuries it was a place for gossip and gambling as well as for cures for gout.

So visit the remains of the monumental Roman baths and temple, linger in the eighteenth-century Pump Room to taste the water, look at the spectacular fan vaulting in the medieval abbey, explore the narrow passageways of the city centre and enjoy strolling along the wide pavements of the Georgian streets. Above all enjoy the atmosphere of a city that has had an enduring appeal since Roman times.

BELOW **Viewed from Beechen Cliff, Bath appears a golden city set within surrounding green hills.**

History

Bath is a Georgian city *par excellence* but it has been shaped by two thousand years of history, and fascinating remains of this long and varied past are still visible today.

It was established as a town soon after the Roman invasion of Britain in AD 43. This was a walled town, and the line of the Roman walls, which were adopted and rebuilt in the Middle Ages, survives today in the route and names of two roads in the city centre, Upper and Lower Borough Walls.

The town was famous in Roman times for its baths and adjoining temple. Indeed, Roman Bath was called Aquae Sulis – the waters of Sulis in honour of the Celtic goddess already worshipped at the spring.

According to legend, Bladud founded Bath in 863 BC. Although heir to the throne, his leprosy was so bad that he was banished to keep pigs in the Avon valley. One day, as the pigs emerged from a steamy swamp, their skin diseases were found to have gone, and so Bladud discovered the cure for his own leprosy. Returning to court, he in time became king and founded the city and the thermal baths. His statue now presides over the King's Bath.

The temple and baths, developed over nearly four centuries of Roman rule, were so impressive that hundreds of years later a Saxon poet marvelled at the remains: '. . . the buildings raised by giants are crumbling, the roofs have collapsed, the towers are in ruins. There stood courts of stone

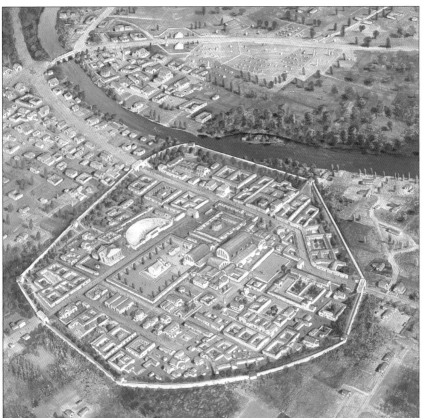

LEFT **Bath – Aquae Sulis – as it might have appeared in later Roman Britain. The baths, with vaulted roofs, dominate the centre of the town. Alongside, surrounded by a precinct wall, is the temple dedicated to Sulis Minerva. The line of the walls, preserved in Bath's later street plan, shows that despite the fame of the baths and temple this was a very small Roman town.**

and a stream gushing forth in rippling floods of hot water.' It is obvious why the Saxons named the town Bath. The excavated Roman ruins – hidden for centuries – are today just as evocative of the past grandeur.

The founding of a monastery in Bath brought renewed fame. The coronation of the first king of England, Edgar, took place in the abbey church in 973 in the presence of Dunstan, Archbishop of Canterbury, and Oswald, Archbishop of York. After the Norman Conquest, Bath Abbey became a cathedral and was rebuilt on a grand scale. The present church, dating from 1499, was one of the last great churches to be built before the Reformation.

The loss of the great monastery, closed by Henry VIII in the 1530s, was a temporary setback to Bath's fortunes. But by the seventeenth century the curative waters had once again become the main reason to visit the city. James I's queen,

LEFT **This bronze head of Minerva, the Roman goddess of wisdom and healing, was found in 1727 by workmen digging a sewer beneath Stall Street close to Abbey Church Yard. The beautiful head survives from a cult statue used in the Roman temple on that site and is now on display in the Roman Baths Museum.**

ABOVE **The Romans had a sophisticated underfloor heating system in the baths. Brick** *pilae* **allowed hot air to circulate in this hypocaust system.**

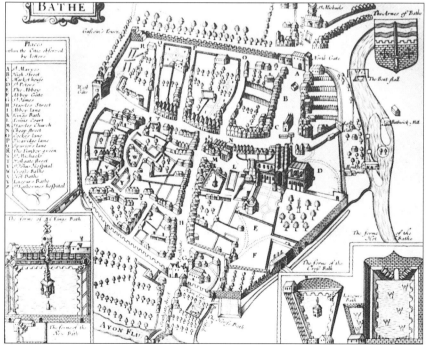

LEFT **John Speed's 1610 map records Bath as it was at the end of the Middle Ages. The abbey has replaced the baths as the city's main building, but the walls follow the same course and there is little suburban expansion.**

Anne of Denmark, came to Bath
three times in search of a cure
for her dropsy, and later in the
century two more queens of England
came in the hope that the effects of

the water would aid the conception
of a child. In the case of Mary, wife of
James II, it appeared to have helped
– with momentous consequences.
The birth of a Catholic heir to the

LEFT **Thomas Rowlandson's drawings of** *The Comforts of Bath* **show the less decorous side of eighteenth-century society in search of a cure. This is one of the series of cartoons which depict the gouty admirals, the old and the infirm in energetic pursuit of good health.**

throne led directly to the Glorious Revolution and the abdication of King James.

The presence of Queen Anne did much to promote Bath as a fashionable resort at the start of the eighteenth century. This it remained for the next hundred years, as its population grew from 2,000 in 1700 to 28,000 in 1801. The extra people were housed in the elegant new buildings which extended the city up the surrounding hillsides and across the river. They were entertained in impressive public buildings which remain in use to this day: the Pump Room, the baths, the Assembly Rooms and the Guildhall.

Visitors and residents in the eighteenth century constitute a *Who's Who* of English life. Bath was at times home to military and naval men including General Wade, Wolfe of Quebec and Lord Nelson; the politician William Pitt; writers Jane Austen, Dr Johnson, Richard Sheridan, Henry Fielding and Samuel Richardson; the artist Thomas Gainsborough; and numerous aristocrats and members of the royal family.

In truth, the great events of their lives often took place away from Bath. The city was known as a seasonal resort and later as a place of retirement, but this by no means diminishes its greatness. Bath has attracted visitors throughout history, and in recent years the revealing of the Roman remains and the cleaning of the Georgian buildings has revived its claim to be considered among the most beautiful cities in Europe.

Bath has given its name to a bun, a biscuit and an invalid chair. The Bath bun is a round, spiced currant bun with icing, not to be confused with the famous Sally Lunn, an uniced bun, also baked in Bath. In contrast, the Bath Oliver is a plain, unsweetened biscuit invented in the eighteenth century by Dr William Oliver, co-founder of the Royal Mineral Water Hospital, Bath, as part of his treatment for overweight patients. The Bath chair is a type of wheelchair favoured by invalids and was a familiar sight on the streets of Bath in the last century.

Baths and Pump Room

BELOW **The Great Bath is the impressive centrepiece of the Roman bathing complex. The swimming pool is still lined with fourteen great sheets of lead from the Mendip Hills, and the bases of the columns that supported a domed roof are still visible, surrounded by the colonnade and statues built at the time of Victorian excavations.**

The Roman citizen relaxing in one of the warm rooms in the baths and the Georgian squire's wife floating in the Queen's Bath had this in common: they believed that this activity was good for their health and they enjoyed the opportunity it provided for gossip.

In both these periods bathing had become a ritual. In the Roman baths it involved sitting in a succession of increasingly hot rooms and having the dirt scraped off the skin before sealing the pores by plunging into a cold bath. In such a large bathing complex there was also a place for exercises and, of course, the Great Bath for swimming.

In Georgian England the time for bathing was early in the morning. After arriving by sedan chair, visitors would be helped into capacious bathing clothes by an attendant before wallowing in the warm water

for up to an hour. Then, the wet bathing clothes removed, they would return to their lodgings wrapped in blankets to go back sweating to bed. Once they were cooled, it would be time to go out to breakfast.

After breakfast came the social ritual masquerading as health cure: the visit to the Pump Room to drink the recommended three glasses of mineral water and to mix with the other visitors to Bath. Thereafter, for the rest of the day, the social round moved away from the baths and Pump Room – to coffee houses,

RIGHT This is the remains of one of several cold plunge baths. Having spent time soaking and steaming in a series of hot baths, the Roman bather would plunge into cold water to seal the pores of the skin before dressing and leaving.

ABOVE The King's Bath, for centuries the largest of the city's baths, was once open to public view. Now enclosed by buildings, it can be seen from inside the Pump Room and Roman Baths Museum. The stone benches used by bathers are now visible above the current water level.

LEFT The Stall Street entrance to the Pump Room is marked by an elegant colonnade matching the one leading into Abbey Church Yard. The Pump Room and the colonnades – and much of grand central Bath – were designed by Thomas Baldwin.

LEFT The Pump Room has been the hub of fashionable Bath for two centuries. Designed by Thomas Baldwin in 1789 and built on the site of an earlier pump room, it is decorated by giant Corinthian columns inspired by Roman architecture.

BELOW The trio ensures a graceful atmosphere in the Pump Room on weekday mornings and Sunday afternoons.

Richard 'Beau' Nash is, more than anyone, associated with Bath's rise as a fashionable resort in the early eighteenth century. As Master of Ceremonies for over fifty years, he laid down a set of rules governing social activities in the city, for example banning the wearing of swords and duelling, and thus ensured that Bath gained the reputation of being a safe and civilised place. A wit, womaniser, gambler and benefactor, Nash was not without his faults, but he had an important and positive part to play in the story of Bath. His statue watches benignly over activities in the Pump Room.

reading rooms, a service in the abbey and a promenade along the Parades, followed by dinner, a game of cards and dancing in one of the assembly rooms.

How efficacious was the water? The judgement of modern medicine has been harsh, yet the wisdom of

LEFT Mineral water can still be drunk from this fountain in the Pump Room, though Dickens's Sam Weller thought it had 'a wery strong flavour o' warm flat irons'.

LEFT The Cross Bath is once again open as a place to relax – but not yet to swim.

FAR LEFT The Romans venerated the source of the hot water as a sacred spring – but they also made practical use of it. Their reservoir which stored water from the spring is now hidden under the King's Bath, but the overflow to the reservoir is still visible.

centuries indicates the remarkable qualities of this warm mineral water. Many of the approaches used in Bath until recently remain in popular use in the home today, including massages, showers, mud treatment, whirlpool baths and, of course, mineral water for drinking.

Three hot springs emerge close to each other in the centre of Bath, bringing a quarter of a million gallons of water at an average temperature of 47°C to the surface each day. The best known is the spring which fed the Roman baths, and which later served the King's Bath and adjoining Queen's Bath in Georgian times. Since the baths had been constructed one on top of the other over the centuries, it was not until the nineteenth century that excavations revealed the extent of the Roman baths below ground level. The King's Bath can still be seen from the Pump Room; the Queen's Bath was removed in order to reveal the Roman baths below.

A short walk away, the other two springs serve the Cross Bath, of 1784, and the Hot Bath, designed by John Wood the younger in 1776. The Cross Bath, which is open to visitors, provides an opportunity to inspect the warm, murky green water at close hand. There is even talk of reintroducing bathing here in the near future.

LEFT Robert Cruikshank's watercolour showing public bathing in Bath in the early nineteenth century carries the title *Stewing Alive*. Visitors often noted that the water caused them to sweat profusely – partly because of its heat, but also because of its minerals.

Streets, squares and crescents

At the start of the eighteenth century Bath was still largely contained within its ancient walls, and the architect John Wood the elder described the city as retaining a medieval squalor. Within decades it was transformed by a boom which saw the rebuilding of the centre of the city and its expansion to the surrounding hillsides and across the river. The result was the city familiar to visitors today, characterised by elegant streets, squares and crescents and impressive public buildings.

Architect-speculators acquired land for development and then drew up plans for the fronts of the buildings to ensure conformity to an overall scheme. The design of the interior plans and the backs was then left to the individual builders who took on responsibility for completing and selling each building. A glance behind the Circus shows how different each individual building could be.

ABOVE **Cavendish Crescent with Lansdown Crescent behind. These less-often-visited crescents on the Lansdown slopes make good use of the dramatic landscape. John Betjeman considered the sequence of Lansdown Crescent and adjoining Somerset Place as 'without equal as a spectacular townscape'.**

BELOW **The dominant north side of Queen Square was designed by John Wood the elder to resemble a single grand house. The central pediment and corner pavilions help disguise the fact that this is a row of seven town houses.**

The name John Wood occurs more often than any other in a discussion of the appearance of eighteenth-century Bath. Prior Park, Queen Square, the Circus, Royal Crescent and the Assembly Rooms were all designed by John Wood – but in reality this is an architectural dynasty. John Wood the elder (ABOVE) set the tone by declaring his intention to turn Bath into a Roman city, while his son John Wood the younger surpassed even his father's achievement by designing Royal Crescent.

RIGHT **Each house in the Circus parades a wealth of detail: ironwork railings, paired columns for each storey, a decorated frieze above the ground floor and garlands above the second – all topped with ornate stone acorns on the parapet.**

Bath differed from most other cities because of the overall vision of one man, John Wood the elder. His ambition was no less than to create a great Roman-style city complete with forum, circus and gymnasium. In the event his plans were modified, but we are left with North and South Parades as part of his scheme for an imperial forum, or place of assembly, and the Circus, which has been described as resembling the Colosseum turned inside out.

BELOW **From the air, the symmetry of the Circus is revealed: thirty-three houses divided into three blocks by the entry of three evenly spaced streets. Originally the Circus was paved in the centre, creating a great open space. The large plane trees came later.**

RIGHT **Royal Crescent, adorned with 100 columns, is a row of town houses masquerading as a palace. No-one is sure where John Wood the younger gained his inspiration; his crescent was unique in town planning and though later copied in other cities it remains a breathtaking sight.**

BELOW **Many crisply carved and painted original street names are to be found around the city. The elegant Trim Street carving dates from the early eighteenth century.**

Yet Bath remains wholly English. With their extensive schemes John Wood and his son created terraces of town houses in the form of grand country houses, complete with impressive landscape settings. Nowhere is this more evident than in Royal Crescent, designed by John Wood the younger. Here the eye takes in the whole majestic sweep and is barely able to distinguish individual houses, and at the front lawns disappear down the hill as if part of a great landscaped park.

The local limestone had its part to play. Rejected earlier as being too soft for use in London at Greenwich Hospital, Bath stone shows its quality in the local setting. Widespread cleaning of buildings over the last two decades has restored the original golden hue, and the quality of the

BELOW **The ornate stone frieze in the Circus runs along the tops of the Doric columns at ground-floor level, and is decorated with stone carvings representing the arts, the sciences and occupations. The friezes to the other two levels are left plain.**

LEFT Iron snuffers can still be seen beside several Bath doors. They survive from the time when, at night, burning torches carried to guide people through the dark streets would be extinguished at the entrance to the house.

LEFT With regularity demanded from a terrace of Georgian town houses, the doorways provided a rare opportunity to express individuality. As a result there are a great variety of stone surrounds to doors in the city. This one is in Gay Street.

smooth ashlar stonework can be appreciated throughout the city. The typical Bath house has a combination of Welsh slate on the roof, stone façades and wooden doors and sash windows. Sandstone paving stones form a wide pavement outside.

This was a city built for leisure, and these wide pavements are still a pleasure to walk along. Although there are no longer sedan chairs to enable you to take the weight off your feet, the open-top bus provides a popular alternative for today's visitors.

FAR LEFT The iron railings along Lansdown Crescent are extended into ornate lamp holders arching above the entrance to each house. Wrought-iron railings are now painted a uniform black in the city, but would have also been painted blue, grey, stone colour or green in Georgian times.

LEFT Queen Street and Trim Bridge are a pleasingly intimate sight in contrast to Bath's grander streets.

A walk in Bath

This walk, starting in the heart of the city by the abbey and the Roman baths, also takes in the main showpieces of Georgian Bath and provides some spectacular views from the river. The full walk takes about 1½ hours – longer if you visit some of the attractions on the way – but can easily be shortened.

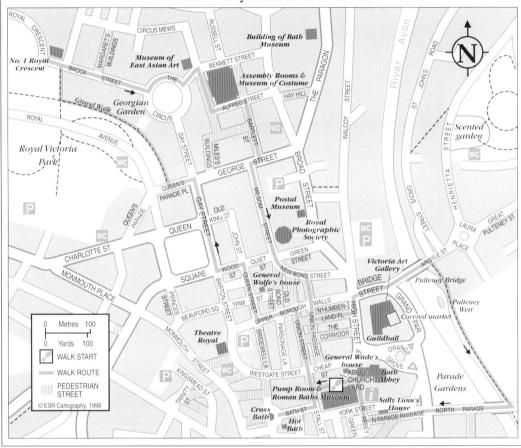

The walk starts in **Abbey Church Yard** (p. 21) *(right)*, with the west front of the abbey dominating the view. As you face the church, to the right is the **Pump Room** (pp. 7, 8) with a Greek motto proclaiming

'Water is Best'. To the left are some charming early-eighteenth-century town houses, notably **General Wade's house** (p. 18) with its impressive Corinthian pilasters, now the National

Trust shop. Turn away from the abbey and through the passage to Stall Street.

A short walk to the left leads to Bath Street *(below)*, which links the city's three historic **hot baths** (pp. 7, 9): the King's Bath, the Hot Bath and the Cross Bath. Retrace your steps to Stall Street and walk on into Union Street. Turn left into Upper Borough Walls, which has remains

of the ancient city walls, and turn right into Queen Street. Walk under **Trim Bridge** (p. 13) *(left)*, with **General Wolfe's house** on the right.

At the top of Queen Street turn left to approach **Queen Square** (p. 10) *(below)*, the first of John Wood the elder's monumental schemes, completed in 1736. Turn right towards the grand north side of the square, and continue along Gay Street. Take

the first turn on the left, Queen's Parade Place, which leads to steps up to Gravel Walk. Follow this path, with views to the left across **Royal Victoria Park** (pp. 22, 23), turning uphill to emerge at **Royal Crescent** (p. 12) *(left)* close to the Bath Preservation Trust's Georgian house, **No. 1 Royal Crescent** (p. 24). The crescent, completed in 1767, was designed by John Wood the younger.

Brock Street leads from Royal Crescent to the elegant **Circus** (p. 11) *(below)*, with thirty-three houses divided into three equal segments. Each is distinguished by the three super-imposed classical orders of architecture. Go to the left and on into Bennett Street, soon turning right past the Assembly Rooms, which houses the

Museum of Costume (pp. 24, 25) and has a restored period ballroom, tea room and card room. Go left along Alfred Street, then right along Bartlett Street.

Cross over to Milsom Street, a short distance to the right, and follow it into New Bond Street, soon crossing over into narrow New Bond Street Place and on into Union Passage. Turn left along Northumberland Place (p. 21), enclosed at the end by a gabled building, and out into High Street opposite the **Guildhall** (pp. 18, 19) *(right)*, which has a splendid banqueting hall.

A short walk to the left brings you to Bridge Street on the right, which leads to shop-lined **Pulteney Bridge** (pp. 20, 22).

Ahead is **Great Pulteney Street** (p. 19) *(below)* leading to the **Holburne Museum** (inside back cover) and **Sydney Gardens** (p. 23), but the walk follows the

steps on the right just after the bridge, leading down to the riverside walk. From here there are splendid views back to Pulteney Bridge *(below)* and across to the abbey. Walk on along the river and take the steps up onto North Parade Bridge. The bridge is a good place to view the city and its surrounding

hillsides. Cross the river and follow the broad pavement of North Parade on the other side. This leads straight into the narrow North Parade Passage, with **Sally Lunn's House** (p. 18) *(right)* on the right. Walk across Abbey Green, the site of the medieval monastic precinct, and then turn right, crossing York Street to return to the abbey.

Bath Abbey

Bath Abbey is a splendid example of late gothic architecture with characteristic fan vaulting and large Perpendicular windows. It is one of the great churches in this English gothic tradition and – begun in 1499 – one of the last to be built before the Reformation.

This rebuilding of the old abbey church was promoted by Bishop Oliver King, who employed the royal master masons Robert and William Vertue who had just completed work on Henry VII's Chapel at Westminster Abbey. They promised Bishop King a splendid vault, saying 'there shall be none so goodely neither in England nor France', and the fan vaulting is indeed the chief glory of the abbey.

But the dissolution of the monasteries brought the role of the abbey to an end in the 1530s, and curtailed the rebuilding. Since then the church has been an abbey only in name, and though it can claim equal billing in the see of Bath and Wells it is not a cathedral, the seat of a bishop, either. Instead, since 1572, the abbey has been the parish church of Bath.

It gained its present appearance only in the nineteenth century when the plaster roof in the nave was replaced with stone fan vaulting to match that in the choir.

Several previous abbey churches have stood on this site. Edgar, the first king of all England, was crowned in an earlier Saxon building. After the Norman Conquest, John of Tours, Bishop of Bath, set out to build a church worthy of its new status as a

BELOW The newly restored west front of the abbey is a tribute to Bishop Oliver King. In a dream he saw angels climbing a ladder to heaven and a voice told him 'Let a king restore the church'. Accordingly he began the complete reconstruction of the abbey in 1499.

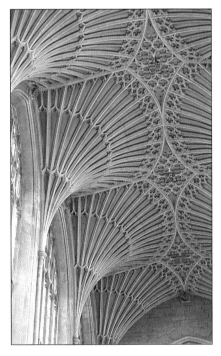

ABOVE **Master masons Robert and William Vertue promised Bishop King the finest vault in England. The result was the spectacular stone fan vault in the eastern arm of the church, matched centuries later when the nave was completed in a similar style.**

RIGHT In a city of restrained Palladian proportions, Bath Abbey stands out in its pinnacled gothic grandeur. The crossing tower, 162 feet (50 m) high, dominates views of Bath by day and by night.

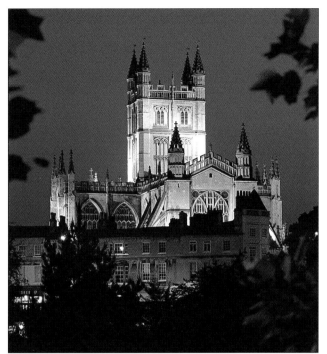

BELOW Prior Birde's chantry chapel, begun in 1515, is a dazzling display of stone carving commemorating the man entrusted with overseeing the rebuilding of the abbey.

ABOVE In his dream Bishop King saw angels ascending and descending a ladder to heaven. To depict the descent, the stonemason carved one of the angels upside down.

LEFT The huge square-headed east window fills the wall at the east end of the abbey. The Victorian stained glass depicts scenes from the life of Christ.

cathedral. This was so large that the present church could have been contained within its nave, with the Norman cathedral's choir extending for another 150 feet (45 m) eastwards across what is now Orange Grove. A few traces of this building remain: the Norman chapel at the east end of the abbey has a round Norman arch surrounding the later Perpendicular window.

Historic buildings

The fame of the baths, the abbey and the streets planned by the Woods is such that Bath's other historic buildings may be overlooked. Yet there is more to see than the great set pieces.

The narrow streets south of the abbey provide reminders of the medieval city, and Sally Lunn's House in North Parade Passage claims to be the oldest house in Bath, despite its seventeenth-century appearance. Excavations in the cellar have shown remains of earlier Roman, Saxon and medieval buildings on this site.

Even before John Wood the elder came to Bath the rebuilding of the city had begun, and impressive early-eighteenth-century townhouses include General Wade's house, now the National Trust shop, in Abbey Church Yard and General Wolfe's house in Trim Street.

One other architect stands out alongside the Woods from Bath's golden age. Thomas Baldwin designed the Guildhall, whose banqueting hall has been described as the finest interior in Bath. It was his town planning that created a new route – colonnaded Bath Street – that

BELOW The National Trust shop occupies a swaggering early-eighteenth-century townhouse in Abbey Church Yard. This was the home of General Wade, MP for Bath, who built the military roads in Scotland to crush Jacobite resistance after the 1715 uprising.

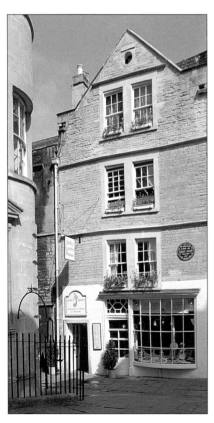

ABOVE **Sally Lunn's House is one of the few houses in the city centre that survived the Georgian rebuilding. It is seventeenth century in appearance, but traces of much earlier buildings have been found in the cellar, which is open to the public.**

THE NATIONAL TRUST

Ralph Allen, known as the 'Man of Bath', was an influential figure in the city's golden age. A self-made man, his fortune came from his organisation of the postal service, then from exploiting the stone quarries on Combe Down which provided much of the stone from which the city was built. Indeed, he commissioned John Wood the elder to design Prior Park to display the virtues of Bath stone. A benevolent figure, he kept an open house for his many friends and acquaintances, and was turned by one into a kindly pen portrait as Squire Allworthy in Henry Fielding's *Tom Jones*.

linked the three thermal baths. He designed the Pump Room – though he was dismissed by the corporation before its completion for failing to submit his accounts – and he was also responsible for planning the Bathwick estate across Pulteney Bridge. Great Pulteney Street, 1,000 feet (300 m) long and 100 feet (30 m) wide and culminating in the Holburne Museum, is an impressive sight indeed.

Other buildings – historic and whimsical – are visible on the skyline from the city. Ralph Allen's great country house, Prior Park, can be

ABOVE The banqueting hall is the grandest room in the Guildhall, home of the city council. Built in the 1770s by Thomas Baldwin, it is in the decorative style introduced by Robert Adam and is adorned with portraits of famous Bath citizens from the eighteenth century. With its large proportions, musicians' gallery and spectacular chandeliers, it was designed for formal banquets.

seen on the slopes across the river, as can his gothic folly, Sham Castle, which was designed to be seen from his town house in North Parade Passage. To the north, the antiquarian William Beckford built an imposing Greek-style tower on Lansdown.

LEFT Opened in 1805, Bath's theatre was known as the 'New' Theatre Royal because it followed earlier playhouses in the city. Rebuilt internally after a fire in 1862, the building still displays its original grand front to Beauford Square.

Street life and shopping

Bath is one of the most lively of English cities. It has been called a museum city, but if it is then it is a very animated museum boasting a variety of street entertainments, pavement cafés and a multitude of specialist shops.

Indeed, alongside the major monuments the great pleasure of the city is its vivacious street life. Many visitors are content to explore the shops, to relax in a pavement café, and to be entertained by the various street musicians and performers.

Bath's shops are sensibly arranged. Large shops and department stores are on the main north–south axis of the city – in Milsom Street, Union

BELOW **Pulteney Bridge is the only bridge in England completely lined with shops. Though grand in design it is small in its proportions and contains some of Bath's most charming and characteristic small shops.**

ABOVE **Bath's street entertainers add colour to the city's street life, and no one should be surprised to encounter the sight and sound of an eighteenth-century musician.**

BELOW **Stall Street, bright with flowers in summer and with the colonnade leading into Abbey Church Yard, is Bath's main pedestrian shopping street. Rebuilt in the eighteenth century and made fashionable by its shops, there is no visible clue that this was once the site of the Roman temple.**

Street and Stall Street. Boutiques and souvenir shops cluster in the narrow streets and passages to the north of the abbey, while the focus for Bath's many antiques shops is the Lansdown slopes around the Assembly Rooms.

As it has been for centuries, Abbey Church Yard is the focal point of the city – the place to see and be seen. It is large enough to provide a range of musical and theatrical diversions, but small enough to act as a reliable meeting point between shopping excursions.

The wide pavements and numerous pedestrian streets, the many cafés and the relaxed atmosphere of the city mean that it is a particular pleasure to shop, or simply stroll, in Bath.

LEFT Northumberland Place, closed by a gabled seventeenth-century building, is perhaps the most colourful of the city's shopping passageways.

Richard Sheridan's famous comedies *The Rivals* and *School for Scandal*, still enjoyed by theatre audiences today, are both set in Bath. And it was in the city that an episode in Sheridan's own life had the quality of a drama. He, like so many others, had fallen in love with the beautiful singer Elizabeth Linley, and in 1772, when he was twenty-one and she eighteen, they eloped from her house in Royal Crescent to France. Their marriage was kept secret from her father and duels with another admirer followed. Sheridan went on to success as a theatre proprietor in London; sadly, Elizabeth died young of tuberculosis.

ABOVE Abbey Church Yard is the heart of Bath – as it has been for 2,000 years. Lined on one side with cafés and surrounded by historic buildings, it is the place where crowds congregate to watch the many street entertainers.

LEFT Summer in Bath is characterised by hanging baskets and open-air cafés, which give a continental atmosphere to this most English of cities. The fashion for street life has now taken hold, and throughout the year it is possible to find people sitting at outside tables.

River and gardens

Bath is contained within a tight curve of the Avon, so nowhere in the city centre is far from the river. Shop-lined Pulteney Bridge, designed by Robert Adam, was completed in 1770 to allow the city to expand on the other bank.

Parade Gardens are the closest pleasure gardens to the city centre, and provide an elegant place to relax against the backdrop of Bath Abbey while listening to a summertime concert in the bandstand.

The most spacious garden is Royal Victoria Park, named after Princess Victoria who visited the city in 1830 before she became queen. There are outstanding views of Royal Crescent from this park, which also has Bath's botanical garden. Nearby, a Georgian garden has been reconstructed along Gravel Walk between Queen Square and Royal Crescent to show the layout and typical plants grown in a town garden of the period.

RIGHT Designed by Robert Adam and constructed in 1770, Pulteney Bridge is an elegant adornment to the city. Though built in the grand style with three arches and with shops on both sides, it is in fact surprisingly small in scale.

LEFT From North Parade Bridge there is an impressive view of the river, of Pulteney Bridge and of the crescents on Lansdown. This is the place to take a river trip – or simply to enjoy a relaxing stroll in summer.

Jane Austen was a frequent visitor to Bath, and her first novel, *Northanger Abbey*, was largely set in the city. In 1801 she moved to Bath when her father retired as rector of Steventon, Hampshire, and she lived in the city for the next five years. Her last novel, *Persuasion*, was also partly set in Bath. Though the heroines of both books find love in the city, it would appear that Jane Austen herself found Bath rather dull.

LEFT There are spectacular views of the abbey and the river from the centrally located Parade Gardens. The deckchairs, bandstand and immaculate floral borders show that Bath has not forgotten its origins as an elegant resort.

LEFT Royal Victoria Park, covering 57 acres, is the city's largest and most popular open space. Originally planned as an arboretum, it contains many mature trees and a botanical garden as well as spacious lawns.

Across Pulteney Bridge there are two notable parks. Henrietta Park has a small scented garden for blind people, and Sydney Gardens, beyond the Holburne Museum, were laid out in the late eighteenth century. Though planned as a romantic landscape, their most striking features came soon after when the Kennet and Avon Canal and then the Great Western Railway were cut across them. The canal, which was built to allow the transport of goods between the Avon and the Thames, is an attractive addition.

Jane Austen went to a concert in Sydney Gardens, though she looked forward to it, she wrote, because 'the gardens are large enough for me to get pretty well beyond the reach of its sound'.

ABOVE The Kennet and Avon Canal passes through Sydney Gardens, enhancing the earlier landscaped park by the addition of pretty footbridges.

Museums

While much of historic Bath can be enjoyed from the street, a fuller appreciation of the city's past life can be gained by an indoors exploration of its historic buildings and museums.

The **Roman Baths Museum** is a must for every visitor, for it shows the great Roman remains which were revealed over the last two centuries by excavation. Here you can sense the grandeur of the Roman baths, including the Great Bath still lined with 8½ tons of Mendip lead, marvel at the remains of the temple complex, including the Gorgon's head from the temple pediment, and gain a glimpse into distant lives through the objects thrown into the sacred spring as offerings for the gods.

Several great interiors of eighteenth-century Bath are also regularly open to visitors, including the **Pump Room**, the **Guildhall**, the **Assembly Rooms** and **No. 1 Royal Crescent**, restored by the Bath Preservation Trust to show how a Georgian town house might have appeared when first occupied.

Insights into life in Georgian Bath can be gained in the **Victoria Art Gallery**, which contains Bath scenes painted by the topographical artist Thomas Malton as well as paintings by national and European artists, and the fascinating **Building of Bath Museum**, which shows through

ABOVE
The Gorgon's head which once adorned the pediment of Bath's Roman temple is now in the Roman Baths Museum. Curiously, it is not the female head of conventional Roman mythology, with snakes in place of hair, but a wild-eyed Celtic man complete with moustaches.

detailed reconstructions how this architectural masterpiece of a city was built.

Bath also has exhibitions that reflect the wider world. The **Museum of Costume** has displays of fashionable historic and contemporary dress, including a dress from the 1660s as well as outfits from the world's fashion

RIGHT The Roman Baths Museum displays many finds from the Roman town. This grieving face is thought to be a theatrical mask from a tomb.

LEFT Offerings to the gods were thrown into the sacred spring in the Roman baths. These included coins, jewellery and even an inscription cursing a rival for the loss of a girlfriend. They are on display in the Roman Baths Museum.

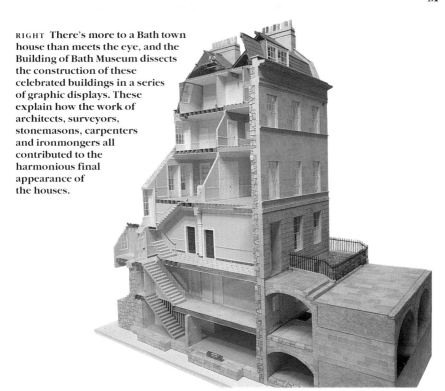

RIGHT **There's more to a Bath town house than meets the eye, and the Building of Bath Museum dissects the construction of these celebrated buildings in a series of graphic displays. These explain how the work of architects, surveyors, stonemasons, carpenters and ironmongers all contributed to the harmonious final appearance of the houses.**

As a portrait painter of the fashionable, it is not surprising that Thomas Gainsborough chose to live and work in Bath. Over fourteen years in his studio in the Circus he painted the celebrated residents and visitors to the city in a style that now seems to characterise the age. His Bath subjects included the singer Elizabeth Linley, the actress Sarah Siddons and the novelists Laurence Sterne and Samuel Richardson. Works by Gainsborough, pictured above in a self-portrait, can be seen at the Holburne Museum in the city.

capitals. Two miles (3.2 km) from the city centre, the **American Museum in Britain** recreates the life of the American settlers, and its displays include period furnished rooms.

Other museums tell the story of some of the extraordinary and eccentric individuals who have lived in Bath. Notable among these, the **Herschel Museum** commemorates the Bath musician William Herschel whose hobby was astronomy. With his home-made telescope he discovered a new planet, Uranus, and was later appointed court astronomer by George III.

LEFT **The Museum of Costume in the Assembly Rooms is an extensive and prestigious collection of fashionable dress, with displays spanning the last four centuries. At any one time 200 dressed figures and up to 1,000 items of costume and jewellery are on display from the collection given to the city in 1963.**

Festivals

Bath's particular appeal over the centuries has been that it is fun to visit. This remains as true today as ever, with the city's historic buildings providing an ideal setting for all sorts of entertainment.

The celebrated Bath International Music Festival, which takes place in late May and early June each year, is traditionally marked by free opening night celebrations in Royal Victoria Park involving fireworks, music and a hot-air balloon fiesta. The programme of classical, jazz and contemporary music performed by international

RIGHT The Bath International Music Festival begins in spectacular fashion with a free opening night firework display in Royal Victoria Park, with Royal Crescent forming an elegant backdrop to the celebrations. After this explosive start the festival provides more than two weeks of classical, jazz and contemporary music supported by the visual arts, walks, talks and a host of free entertainments on the streets and in the city's parks.

LEFT A balloon fiesta accompanies the Bath International Music Festival's opening celebrations. At other times of the year hot-air balloon trips are offered to the public from Royal Victoria Park – an exciting, if daunting, way to see the city, with the promise of a safe and stable platform for taking aerial photographs.

LEFT **This
colourful medieval
tournament on
the lawns in front
of Royal Crescent
is the sort of open-
air attraction
offered alongside
the Bath Inter-
national Music
Festival.**

<small>BELOW</small> **Bath's
historic buildings
provide the perfect
setting for classical
music recitals. The
banqueting hall of
the Guildhall is a
favoured venue
for concerts
during the Bath
International
Music Festival and
during the autumn
Mozartfest.**

artists is combined with walks, talks, comedy and contemporary art exhibitions. Events take place in the city's historic buildings – or simply in the street.

In the second half of the year the Mozartfest provides an annual celebration of Mozart's music. Many of the performances take place in the appropriately elegant eighteenth-century settings of the Assembly Rooms and the Guildhall. Though Mozart never visited Bath, he greatly admired the compositions of his young contemporary, Thomas Linley of Bath (whose sister, a celebrated singer, eloped with the playwright Sheridan). Unfortunately Linley was unable to live up to his early promise as a composer, as he died at the age of twenty-two.

While most visitors still arrive in summer, Bath is more than a seasonal resort. At all times of the year there is something of a festival atmosphere in the city, with concerts, plays, shops, museums and exhibitions providing year-round interest and entertainment.

Further information

BELOW **At the American Museum in Britain, period furnished rooms help recreate early American life.**

Details are correct at the time of writing but may be changed.

American Museum in Britain

Museum dedicated to early American history and life with eighteen period furnished rooms.

Claverton Manor, Claverton Down, 2 miles (3.2 km) from Bath (Tel. 01225 460503). Open end Mar–early Nov Tue–Fri 1–6, Sat and Sun 12–6, bank hol Sun and Mon 11–5; grounds 11–6. Admission charge.

Bath Abbey

Open Apr–Oct Mon–Sat 9–6, Nov–Mar Mon–Sat 9–4.30, Sun all year 1.15–2.30, 4.30–5.30. Admission free (donations invited).

Beckford's Tower

Monument to the eccentric collector William Beckford, with panoramic views.

Lansdown Road, 1.5 miles (2.4 km) from city centre (Tel. 01225 338727). Note that Beckford's Tower is closed at present but is scheduled to reopen in 1999.

RIGHT **Silver-gilt 'bell' salt and cover (London, 1613) displayed in the Holburne Museum, Great Pulteney Street.**

Book Museum

Display of antiquarian books and bookbinding.

Manvers Street (Tel. 01225 466000). Open Mon–Fri 9–1 and 2–5.30, Sat 9.30–1. Admission charge.

Building of Bath Museum

Displays the development of the Georgian Bath, showing design, building and decoration. The exhibits include full-size reconstructions, artefacts, tools and models.

The Countess of Huntingdon's Chapel, The Vineyards, The Paragon (Tel. 01225 333895). Open mid-Feb–end Nov Tue–Sun and bank holiday Mon 10.30–5. Admission charge.

Cross Bath

Eighteenth-century baths, which are now a quiet retreat in the city centre.

Bath Street. Open Fri–Sun 11.30–5.30. Admission free (donations invited).

Georgian Garden

Reconstructed town garden showing the layout of around 1770 with typical plants of the period.

Gravel Walk (Tel. 01225 477760). Open May–Oct Mon–Fri 9–4.30, Aug also Sun 2–6. Admission free.

Guildhall

The seat of city government, with a splendid first-floor banqueting hall.

High Street (Tel. 01225 477782). Banqueting hall open Mon–Fri 8.30–5 unless it has been reserved for an event. Admission free.

Herschel Museum

The period home of astronomer Sir William Herschel (1738–1822).

New King Street (Tel. 01225 311342). Open Mar–Oct daily 2–5, Nov–Feb Sat and Sun 2–5. Admission charge.

ABOVE The Holburne Museum displays Old Masters alongside contemporary art and craft.

Holburne Museum and Crafts Study Centre

Displays of eighteenth- and twentieth-century art and crafts. *Great Pulteney Street (Tel. 01225 466669). Open mid Feb–mid Dec Mon–Sat 11–5 (June–Sept. opens 10.30; Nov–Easter closed Mon), Sun 2.30–5.30. Admission charge.*

Mr Bowler's Business

(Bath Industrial Heritage Centre) The Victorian workshops of the firm J.B. Bowler & Sons, who were engineers and manufacturers of fizzy drinks. *Julian Road (Tel. 01225 318348). Open Easter–Oct daily 10–5, Nov–Easter Sat and Sun 10–5. Admission charge.*

Museum of Costume and Assembly Rooms

Collection of historic and contemporary dress in Bath's Assembly Rooms. *Bennett Street (Tel. 01225 477782). Open all year Mon–Sat 10–5, Sun 11–5. Admission charge.*

Museum of East Asian Art

Ancient and modern art from east Asia. *Bennett Street (Tel. 01225 464640).*

Open Apr–Oct Mon–Sat 10–6, Sun 10–5, Nov–Mar Mon–Sat 10–5, Sun 12–5. Admission charge.

No. 1 Royal Crescent

Recreated eighteenth-century domestic interiors. *Royal Crescent (Tel. 01225 428126). Open Feb–Nov Tue–Sun 10.30–5 and bank hol. Mon. Admission charge.*

Postal Museum

Presentation of the history of the postal system. *Broad Street (Tel. 01225 460333). Open Mon–Sat 11–5, Sun 2–5. Admission charge.*

ABOVE This model of a mailcoach is from the Postal Museum, which tells the story of the postal system since the days of Henry VIII.

Prior Park

A fine example of an English eighteenth-century landscape garden by 'Capability' Brown, offering panoramic views of the city and a one-mile walk. Owned by the National Trust. *(Tel. 01225 833422). Open Wed–Mon 12.00–5.30 (or dusk, if earlier). Closed 25, 26 Dec and New Year's Day. NOTE: There is no parking at or near Prior Park; public transport is available. Admission charge.*

Pump Room

Originally the place to drink the mineral water and socialise,

now a popular restaurant. *Stall Street (Tel. 01225 444477). Open daily 9.30–6, Sun 10.30–5 (restaurant daily 9.30–5.30 summer, Mon–Sat 9.30–4/4.30, Sun 10.30–4/4.30 winter).*

Roman Baths Museum

The most impressive Roman baths and temple complex in Britain, with finds from two centuries of excavations. *Stall Street (Tel. 01225 477782). Open Apr–Sep 9–6 (Aug also 8 pm–10 pm); Oct–Mar Mon–Sat 9.30–5, Sun 10.30–5. Admission charge.*

Royal Photographic Society

International photographic exhibitions in the Octagon. *The Octagon, Milsom Street (Tel. 01225 462841). Open daily 9.30–5.30. Admission charge.*

Sally Lunn's Kitchen Museum

Cellar kitchen where the famous buns were baked. *North Parade Passage (Tel. 01225 461634). Open Mon–Sat 10–6, Sun 11–6 (dinner from 6 pm daily). Admission charge.*

Tourist Information Centre

Advice on accommodation, events and guided tours. *Abbey Chambers, Abbey Church Yard (Tel. 01225 477101). Open Mon–Sat 9.30–5, Sun 10–4, extended hours in summer. (These opening hours are subject to change.)*

Victoria Art Gallery

Bath's city art gallery, with collections of paintings and decorative arts of local and international interest. *Bridge Street (Tel. 01225 477772). Open Mon–Fri 10–5.30, Sat 10–5. Admission free.*